CREATIVE times WITH GOD

discovering NEW WAYS to connect with the SAVIOR

D1550607

cre·ate (P) Pronunciation (kr-t)
tr.v. cre·at·ed, cre·at·ing, cre·ate:
1. To cause to exist;
bring into being. *2.* To
give rise to; produce *3.*
To produce through

DOUG Fields

(⊙) simply for students

Creative Times with God
Discovering New Ways to Connect with the Savior

Copyright © 2009 Doug Fields

group.com
simplyyouthministry.com

Credits
Executive Developer: Nadim Najm
Chief Creative Officer: Joani Schultz
Copy Editor: Rob Cunningham
Cover Art and Production: Veronica Lucas
Production Manager: DeAnne Lear

ISBN 978-0-7644-6298-6

15 14 13 12 11   20 19 18 17 16

Printed in the United States of America.

Dedicated to the three greatest children in the world:
Torie, Cody, & Cassie Fields

My prayer is that you would have great times with your
Savior as you continue to grow and follow Jesus.

Table of Contents

introduction

I thought I'd made a big mistake when I asked some teenagers in my youth group what they thought about the Bible.

- "The Bible is boring."
- "The Bible is too hard to understand."
- "Why do I have to read the Bible every day at the same time?"
- "I'd rather eat pizza than do a Bible study."

After hearing these negative responses, I decided to dig a little deeper and ask some direct questions. I'm glad I did! What I discovered was that our teenagers really did want to read and understand God's Word; they just needed some help. **They wanted a practical resource that would help and guide them to Bible passages they could understand.** They wanted questions that would trigger them to think about how the Bible connects to them in the 21st century. They wanted something more than open Bible, read Bible, close Bible. Basically, they wanted something that would prompt them to be in God's Word that wasn't the same every day.

This little book, *Creative Times With God,* **is one of the results of our discussion.**

Many people enter into a relationship with God with a desire to better understand the Bible. They want to eagerly study it, memorize it, and attempt to live it out. In their early enthusiasm, they look to others for examples of personal Bible study. It's natural for adults to teach the ways they were taught, saying something like, "Have a daily quiet time at the same hour of the day, using the same materials in the same way every day until you develop a habit." The thinking behind this is that a lot of the same equals developing a habit. Once equipped with formats, structures, guidelines, and expectations, eager teenagers dive in. **I love the initial passion!**

But as time passes, they tire of the same routine and start to lose interest. Their Bibles begin to collect dust and they feel guilty for missing their spiritual appointment with God.

Does that sound like you? Do you need a little variety? Would something different each day help you look forward to digging a little deeper into God's Word?

Some of us can do our Bible time the same way at the same time every day—and if that's you, congratulations. But some of us need variety and creativity to keep our quiet times fresh and alive. And that's great too—part of growing deeper in one's faith is to spend time with God through his Word.

Creative Times With God was designed to introduce a little variety into your times with God. I hope the devotional adventures in this book will ignite your creativity and fire up your passion for knowing God more personally and intimately.

My prayer is that these creative moments you'll experience will lead to some "habit-forming" ways to spend time with God on your own.

May you grow more in love with God and his ways and have fun!

—Doug Fields
Lake Forest, California

 # Bank on It

A Christian banker tells you he sees a lot of similarities between his bank and the church. "For example," he says, "with online banking and ATM machines, the bank doesn't need to be open for people to get what they want. In the same way, the church building doesn't need to be open for people to talk to God."

What are some similarities you can think of between the church and the following features of a bank? Add a few of your own that come to mind.

1. The building
2. The money
3. The personnel or staff
4. The vault
5. Interest and/or interest rates
6. The service
7.
8.
9.

Before you finish, read Acts 2:42-47.
Thank God for the local church body you attend, and ask God to bless the leadership there. Pray about ways you can specifically serve at the church.

I Am

In the Gospel of John, Jesus used seven **I am** statements to describe himself and his ministry. Read these **I am** statements and write down what you think Jesus meant by each.

1. John 6:35,41,48,51   I am the_____

2. John 8:12; 9:5   I am the_____

3. John 10:7,9   I am the_____

4. John 10:11,14   I am the_____

5. John 11:25   I am the_____

6. John 14:6   I am the_____

7. John 15:1,5   I am the_____

If Jesus were sitting with you right now in Starbucks, what kind of **I am** statement might he use to describe himself so that you could better understand him? Why?

I am the_____

Would you use the same statements to describe Jesus to your friends and family?

Jesus is_____

4

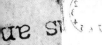# Dead but Alive

Galatians 2:20 reads,

> My old self has been crucified with Christ.
> It is no longer I who live, but Christ
> lives in me. So I live in this earthly
> body by trusting in the Son of God, who
> loved me and gave himself for me.

In the column on the left you will find some incomplete statements based on the above Galatians passage. To complete the statement, connect it with one of the phrases on the right side (simply draw a line that connects it). You will need to think carefully about the meaning of the verse to make the proper match.

My life now...   has no spiritual worth.

My life in Christ...   is lived by faith.

My human body...   is new life.

My faith...   is the giver of life.

My God...   is in Christ.

Rewrite Galatians 2:20 in your own words:

Pick one of the five statements and write a short comment about **what it means to you.**

Take time to express your **thanks in writing** for God's loving sacrifice. Ask God for guidance in your life of faith.

A little extra

What thing or things have to die in your life for you to be alive in Christ? How are you going to kill them?

cre·ate (e) Pronunciation ( )
tr.v. cre·at·ed, cre·at·ing, cre
1. To cause to exist
bring into being. 2. T
give rise to; produce
To produce through

A Friend(ly) Job Description

A job description usually explains the expectations that a boss has for an employee. Job descriptions clarify how employees should behave, dress, and perform.

Read **Proverbs 16:7; 17:9,17; 18:24;** and **27:6,9.** Then write a job description for a good friend, based on these verses. Include specific qualities that outline how a good friend will behave.

`A good friend should...`

According to this job description, are you a **good friend**? Why or why not?

What are some of your **strengths**?

What **could you do this** week to become a better friend?

Think of one of your good friends and take a moment **to pray** for this specific person.

 $hopping $pree

Imagine that you've been given $100 to buy items at a store that sells only qualities, skills, and spiritual gifts. You can spend your money however you want, but shop wisely because there are no returns or exchanges—and you only have **$100.** Circle the items you will buy that total no more than $100. Then answer the questions on the next page.

$90 athletic talent	**$40** sense of humor
$35 encouragement	**$45** forgiveness
$75 singing skills	**$30** self-control
$10 eternal life	**$60** faith
$40 wisdom	**$65** peace
$50 acting ability	**$25** writing skills
$30 patience	**$40** speaking in tongues
$65 future knowledge	**$20** stress management
$30 leadership	**$20** joy
$25 gentleness	**$45** servanthood
$35 communication skills	**$85** ability to heal
$45 organization	**$25** sensitivity
$70 humility	**$35** hope

Why did you select the items you circled?

How would your "purchases" change your life in the future?

Would God choose the same items for you? Why or why not?

How do your selections compare to the list of qualities in Philippians 4:8?

# Praise Report

Psalm 92 is a beautifully written expression of praise to God. Read this psalm and use it as an example for your own personal letter of praise. Take time to tell God why you love him today. Don't ask God for anything in this letter. **Just focus on words of thanksgiving and praise.** Keep this letter as a reminder of God's goodness when life gets tough.

Another option: Go to www.wordle.net. Type "God" or "Jesus" as the primary name and then type as many expressions of those words that you can think of. Take delight in the result and then print out and post it so that it can be seen.

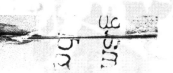

Three-Sixteen

John 3:16 is unquestionably the most popular verse of Scripture in the Bible. We can learn a lot about God's love for us from this one verse. But there are several other "three-sixteens" in the New Testament that also teach us a lot about our Christian faith. Look up each "three-sixteen" below and write it out completely in the space provided.

John 3:16-

1 Corinthians 3:16-

Colossians 3:16-

2 Timothy 3:16-

1 John 3:16-

cre·ate (ɛ) Pronunciation (k
tr.v. cre·at·ed, cre·at·ing, cre
1. To cause to exis
bring into being. 2. T
give rise to; produce
To produce through

A little extra:

Take each verse and rewrite it in a haiku (three lines, with a pattern of five syllables for the first line, seven syllables for the second line, and five syllables for the third line).

[example]

Jesus Son of God
Loves me, knows me, died for me
With him forever

Imagine that these five verses were the only passages of Scripture you had ever read. Write a paragraph below summarizing what you know about the Christian faith from these important "three-sixteens."

Price Check

In 1 Corinthians 6, Paul talks about our physical bodies and the importance of sexual purity. He concludes the chapter by saying that God bought you with a high price. So you must honor God with your body (1 Corinthians 6:20).

How would you rate your response to this biblical command? Put a price on these various elements of your human body between $0 and $100, based on how well they currently honor God. Then list what you view to be your strength and weakness for each element.

Elements	Price	Strength	Weakness
1. Mind			
2. Mouth			
3. Body			
4. Sexuality			
5. Appearance			
6. Personality			

Take time to thank God for paying the price for your life (see Romans 3:23 and 6:23) and for the unique strengths God has given you. If you struggle with relational purity, visit www.xxxchurch.com to get some helpful information, prayer, and resources. Don't put it off.

14

My Significant Other

As Paul worked to spread the good news about Jesus and to establish churches, he apparently enjoyed several significant relationships. Timothy was one young man Paul spent a lot of time with and trained to minister and lead others. Paul called Timothy his **"true son in the faith"** (1 Timothy 1:2). The New Testament letters bearing Timothy's name were written by Paul to encourage him, instruct him, and advise him. Timothy counted on Paul's maturity and wisdom to help him grow and lead others.

Is there an older, wiser, and more mature Christian in your life who could be a "Paul" to you? Is there a younger Christian in your life who might be a "Timothy" to you? Identify these people below.

List some names of people who you'd like to be your "Paul":

List some names of people who you think could become your "Timothy":

List at least three important qualities that should be found in someone who plays the role that Paul played to Timothy:

Sometime today ask a person from your Paul list (above) to consider being a Paul to you.

Wanted!

Imagine that you live in a country where being a follower of Jesus is illegal. You are wanted for questioning by government authorities because you love and believe in Jesus.

Write your name in the blanks on the "WANTED" poster below. Then write a statement explaining what you believe and the reason you are wanted. If you need some help, see Matthew 16:13-16 and 1 Corinthians 15:1-5.

```
                    WANTED
     FOR BEING A FOLLOWER OF JESUS

     _____  _____


          This suspect believes in




```

If you're interested, check out **www.persecution.com** to learn more about what it really means to be persecuted for your faith.

Here's a big step: Consider posting your wanted poster at church, in your room, or on your locker at school.

16

RIPE OR ROTTEN?

RottenTomatoes.com is a website that ranks movies by using **ROTTEN** tomatoes for a bad film and **RIPE** tomatoes for a good film. It's very easy to identify the good from the bad. The Bible has its own fruit section that creates a picture of good, and you can find it in Galatians 5:22-23. These verses list good fruit that God wants to produce in our lives.

Read the passage and list the nine fruit of the Spirit below. Then think through this last week and rate yourself with the word **RIPE** or **ROTTEN** next to fruit of the Spirit that might describe your current life condition. *(Or feel free to draw a picture instead!)*

1.

2.

3.

4.

5.

6.

7.

8.

9.

17

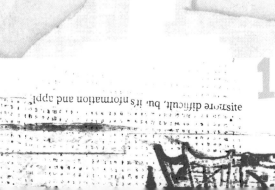

God is Like...

Look around the room and locate an object. Write the name of the object in the blank space on the next page. List in the left column some descriptive qualities of the object. Next to each quality in the right column write how you think God is similar (see the example, "God is like a shoe," below). If possible, find a verse that fits with your description.

There are no right or wrong answers in this exercise. Write down whatever comes to mind. Make sure you take time to thank God for all the special blessings he brings into your life.

Example:

God is like a _Shoe_.   God

1. Protects my feet

1. God protects me (Psalm 91:2)

2. Helps me walk

2. God guides my path and helps me walk in the right direction (Psalm 119:105)

3. Dependable

3. God promises never to leave me (Matthew 28:20)

4. Comes in pairs

4. I am not alone, God gave me his Holy Spirit to always be with me (John 14:16)

5. Many different styles

5. God loves all kinds of different people (Acts 10:34,35)

cre·ate (e) Pronunciation (k   )
tr.v. cre·at·ed, cre·at·ing, cre
1. To cause to exist
bring into being. 2. T
give rise to; produce
To produce throu

God is like a _____.   God

1.   1.

2.   2.

3.   3.

4.   4.

5.   5.

Next, try some of these: Jesus is like...,
My church is like..., Heaven will be like...,
God's love is like....

EXCHANGE STUDENT

Many schools offer exchange programs to countries all over the world. Imagine hosting a teenager who is from a country that has little exposure to Jesus. This student is curious why you go to church and wants answers to the following questions:

1. What **two things** do you like most about your church?

   •

   •

2. What are the three **most important things** in your life right now?

   •

   •

   •

3. If **Jesus** is so great, how are you **like him?**

   •

   •

   •

4. What is **so special** about Jesus?

End your time by reading **Ecclesiastes 12:1** and asking God to make you the person you were created to be.

A little extra:

Pause for a minute and consider your own friends who aren't familiar with Jesus. How might you trigger their curiosity?

Idea: Start a Facebook question thread, tag some friends, and ask for the **top five reasons** that make Jesus great or worth following.

Other Ideas:

Who Accepts Me?

I am afraid to tell you who I am, because, if I tell you who I am, you may not like who I am, and it's all that I have (John Powell, *Why Am I Afraid to Love?*).

1. Do you sometimes feel that if you were totally honest about yourself (your fears, insecurities, failures, and dreams) with someone, that person might not accept you anymore? If so, why?

2. What scares you the most about telling others about your real self?

3. Do you really believe that God accepts you no matter what your "issues" may be? If so, why? If not, why not?

4. Why is acceptance from others so different from God's acceptance?

5. What might you do this week to be more accepting of others?

6. Read **James 5:16** and comment on why James feels it is important for us to confess our sins to one another.

Remember: God accepts you not for what you do (like your friends might) but for who you are, and he won't love you any more or any less than he does right now.

A little extra

Who are you when nobody is looking? What is one way you can be the **same person that God made you to be** when you're alone and when you're around others?

Yes, I'm Positive

Most people crave positive comments from others, but we live in a culture that seems to notice and highlight the negative. While we may love to hear words such as "great job," we often hear things like, "Why didn't you clean up your room?"

Read Matthew 12:33-37 to learn what Jesus had to say about the words we use. Then, in the spaces below, write three sincere, positive comments to three different people in your life. (You choose: parents, teachers, coaches, youth minister, friends, siblings, neighbor, and so on.)

After writing, say a prayer of thankfulness for each person. Then make this exercise even more personal and meaningful by sending a text to each person.

Here's an example of positive comments:

MOM
Thank you for always caring about me even though at times I don't act like I care about you.

You made me feel good the other day when you didn't yell at me for not completing my English assignment. Thanks for being understanding.

You do a great job of making my friends feel comfortable when they come to our house.

cre·ate (e) Pronunciation (k
tr.v. cre·at·ed, cre·at·ing, cre
1. To cause to exist
bring into being. 2. T
give rise to; produce
To produce through

Now, it's your turn! (Try to come up with some different comments than the examples provided.)

Person #1:

Person #2:

Person #3:

Love Notes

In **1 Corinthians 13:1-13** you will find an incredible description of love. Read the chapter in your Bible and list below the qualities of love you find (for an additional description of love, see one from The Message on the next page). Then evaluate the presence of that quality in your life by circling a number between 1 and 10 (1 means that the quality of love is never present; 10 means it is always present). Next, write a brief note for each quality describing how you might improve your rating.

QUALITY	NEVER									ALWAYS
_____	1 2 3 4 5 6 7 8 9 10
_____	1 2 3 4 5 6 7 8 9 10
_____	1 2 3 4 5 6 7 8 9 10
_____	1 2 3 4 5 6 7 8 9 10
_____	1 2 3 4 5 6 7 8 9 10
_____	1 2 3 4 5 6 7 8 9 10
_____	1 2 3 4 5 6 7 8 9 10
_____	1 2 3 4 5 6 7 8 9 10
_____	1 2 3 4 5 6 7 8 9 10
_____	1 2 3 4 5 6 7 8 9 10
_____	1 2 3 4 5 6 7 8 9 10
_____	1 2 3 4 5 6 7 8 9 10
_____	1 2 3 4 5 6 7 8 9 10
_____	1 2 3 4 5 6 7 8 9 10

A little extra

How might you improve one of these qualities? Think of this question in the context of your current relationships. For example: "I will be more patient with my dad" or "I really need to be kinder to my little sister."

If I speak with human eloquence and angelic ecstasy but don't love, I'm nothing but the creaking of a rusty gate. If I speak God's Word with power, revealing all his mysteries and making everything plain as day, and if I have faith that says to a mountain, "Jump," and it jumps, but I don't love, I'm nothing. If I give everything I own to the poor and even go to the stake to be burned as a martyr, but I don't love, I've gotten nowhere. So, no matter what I say, what I believe, and what I do, I'm bankrupt without love.

Love never gives up. Love cares more for others than for self. Love doesn't want what it doesn't have. Love doesn't strut, Doesn't have a swelled head, Doesn't force itself on others, Isn't always "me first, "Doesn't fly off the handle, Doesn't keep score of the sins of others, Doesn't revel when others grovel, Takes pleasure in the flowering of truth, Puts up with anything, Trusts God always, Always looks for the best, Never looks back, But keeps going to the end. Love never dies.

Inspired speech will be over some day; praying in tongues will end; understanding will reach its limit. We know only a portion of the truth, and what we say about God is always incomplete. But when the Complete arrives, our incompletes will be canceled. When I was an infant at my mother's breast, I gurgled and cooed like any infant. When I grew up, I left those infant ways for good. We don't yet see things clearly. We're squinting in a fog, peering through a mist. But it won't be long before the weather clears and the sun shines bright! We'll see it all then, see it all as clearly as God sees us, knowing him directly just as he knows us!

But for right now, until that completeness, we have three things to do to lead us toward that consummation: Trust steadily in God, hope unswervingly, love extravagantly. And the best of the three is love.

1 Corinthians 13:1-13 (MSG)

Growing STRONG

For I can do everything through Christ, who gives me strength (Philippians 4:13).

List your three greatest achievements:

1.

2.

3.

List your three greatest strengths:

1.

2.

3.

Offer thanks for how God made you and what you've been able to accomplish in your life.

What specific things currently keep you from building on these strengths?

**Think of a creative way to thank God
for the strengths you've been given.**

Do you sing?
If so, sing a thank you song to God in the shower.

Are you an athlete?
Repeat Philippians 4:13 over and over as you compete.

Are you a writer?
Write God a love letter. You get the idea…

Powerfully Weak

Three different times I begged the Lord to take it away. Each time he said, "My grace is all you need. My power works best in weakness." So now I am glad to boast about my weaknesses, so that the power of Christ can work through me. That's why I take pleasure in my weaknesses, and in the insults, hardships, persecutions, and troubles that I suffer for Christ. For when I am weak, then I am strong (2 Corinthians 12:8–10).

In the passage above, underline one phrase that is **most meaningful** to you today. Why did you choose that particular phrase?

How does this Scripture relate to the things you listed in the last lesson ("Growing Strong") that **keep you from building on your strengths?**

Write your own honest statement about your weaknesses. Conclude your statement with a prayer describing the growth you would like to see based on the verses from 2 Corinthians 12.

To go up, you have to go down, right?

Try this: As you pray today, go down on your knees. It's a position of humility. Honor God, boast about your weakness, and ask God's Spirit to work in you today.

Gimme Five

Prayer is an important habit to develop as we deepen our faith in Jesus. The Bible shows us many different ways to communicate with God through prayer. Look up the verses in the left column and try to find the match with the different kinds of prayer described in the right column. Once you've made the correct connection, try an experiment and include all five types of prayer in your personal prayer time today.

1 Thessalonians 5:17	thanksgiving: Giving thanks for how God works in our lives.
Ephesians 5:20	supplication: Asking God to fill our need for something; making a request of God.
Philippians 4:6	praise: Expressing how great and good God is; appreciating God's character.
1 John 1:9	confession: Stating our sins and failures openly to God in order to receive forgiveness.
Psalm 34:3; 150:2	conversation: Communicating with God naturally and continually.

cre·ate ( ) Pronunciation ( )
tr.v. cre·at·ed, cre·at·ing, cre
1. To cause to exis
bring into being. 2. T
give rise to; produce
To produce throug

One of Your Favorites

Write your `favorite Bible verse` on a small piece of paper.
(If you don't have a favorite, select a verse from this book.) Place
the verse in a location where you will see it and think about it
throughout the day (taped to your notebook, your shoe, your
steering wheel, or some other spot you'll see it frequently).

Read your verse often and pray, "Lord, what do you want me to
learn from this verse today?" Before you go to bed, write down
what God might want to teach you and how it might relate to
your life in the days ahead. When you wake up, if you dreamt
about it, make sure you write that down somewhere to reflect
on what that might mean.

Today's verse:

What God taught me about this verse:

Blind Insight

Before you read today's Bible passage, try this experiment: With your eyes closed, perform one of your regular morning activities (getting dressed, eating breakfast, brushing your teeth, or making your bed). Try to simulate the experience of total **blindness** for several minutes.

After your experience without sight, read **Mark 8:22-26.** Pause. Think about this passage. Read it again, this time slowly. When you're finished, look through a newspaper or magazine until you find an image of someone who is **blind** or who experiences another type of physical limitation (for example, someone who needs a stretcher, a wheelchair, or a cane).

Cut out the picture and mount it on the next page. What could you do today to minister to someone in need like Jesus ministered to the **blind** man? Write it down in the space around it. Some ideas might include writing an encouraging letter to someone, visiting a sick friend in the hospital, or taking cookies to an elderly person in a nursing home. **Decide on one ministry activity and carry it out within the next week.**

After completing your task, thank God for your physical sight and your current health and ask God to increase your sensitivity to those in need. Consider what you and/or your youth group might be able to do on a regular basis to help meet the needs of the **blind**, elderly, or disabled in your community.

Where's the Match

Look up the verses in the left column and draw a line from each to its corresponding meaning in the right column. Read each carefully and pick the one that impresses you most. Take a minute to pray and ask God how he wants you to respond in a specific way today or this week.

Matthew 7:1-5   Confess your sins to one another

Romans 6:6-11   God offers unconditional love

John 3:16   Christ now lives in me

James 5:16   Avoid spiritual mediocrity

Revelation 3:16   Jesus died for our sins

Galatians 2:20   Check out your own life before
                       you judge

A little extra

Write down the verse that strikes you the hardest or seems clearest that it might be a verse "for you." **Use your cell phone to take a picture of that verse from your Bible and turn it into your screen saver until you've memorized it.**

36

 # SIMCITY

SimCity was one of the earliest city-building simulation games that allowed players to create cities that looked and functioned the way players believed they should. A healthy foundation for a good city (or team or business) requires excellent leadership. Imagine you've been given a chance to create your own church. What leaders would you want to be on your team?

Read 1 Timothy 3:1-13 and Titus 1:6-9 and write down the biblical qualities for church leaders. List each in the left column and then write the name of an individual you live with, work with, or go to school with who you believe best exemplifies each particular quality. **Be sure to write notes to the people to let them know about your observation of their lives** (encouragement is a great quality).

Pastoral Qualities   Leaders

1.   1.

2.   2.

3.   3.

4.   4.

5.   5.

Fishing Your Crowd

Jesus understood what kind of language to use when communicating with a particular audience. When he was choosing his first disciples, he came upon some fishermen, and his verbal invitation to follow him was spoken in terms they would clearly understand. *Jesus called out to them, "Come, follow me, and I will show you how to fish for people!" And they left their nets at once and followed him (Mark 1:17–18).*

How would you describe the types of audiences you have the opportunity to reach at your school?

What kind of "language" do you need to speak in order to reach them?

cre·ate ( ) Pronunciation (
tr.v. cre·at·ed, cre·at·ing, cre
1. To cause to exist
bring into being. 2. T
give rise to; produce
To produce through

What specific things might you need to do to reach them?

Identify by name the group that you will attempt to reach out to this week. What is one thing you can do to be like Jesus to this group this week?

Putting the Romans Together

The four sentences below are from **Romans 5:20-21**, but they are listed in an incorrect order. Before reading the passage in your Bible, read each sentence very carefully, see if you can figure out the correct order, and then number the sentences accordingly.

As you think about the order, jot down what each sentence says to you. Then check your answer by looking up Romans 5:20-21 in the New Living Translation.

___ But as people sinned more and more, God's wonderful **grace** became more **abundant.**

___ God's law was given so that **all people** could see how sinful they were.

___ …resulting in **eternal life through Jesus Christ** our Lord.

___ So just as sin ruled over all people and brought them to death, now God's wonderful grace rules instead, giving us **right standing with God.**

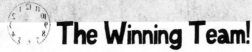

The Winning Team!

The body of Christ (followers of Jesus) can be compared to an athletic team that intends to win. Read **Romans 12:3-8** and **1 Corinthians 12:12-26** to see the description of how followers of Jesus can work together. As you read, list below the similarities between the body of Christ and an athletic team (see the two examples). Be sure to include a verse reference that supports your similarities.

When you finish, **identify two or three people** whom you feel make the body of Christ stronger, and then thank God for them. Consider telling them how valuable they are, too!

Athletic Team	Body of Christ	Scripture
Everyone is talented	God gives gifts to us all	Romans 12:4
Players have different positions	Christians have different gifts	Romans 12:6

Living It Up

Take a few minutes to read **John 3:1-36.** As you read, notice that this passage talks about three types of life: physical life, spiritual life, and eternal life. Answer the following questions as you work through this section of Scripture.

When does each type of life begin?

What do you see as significant about each type
of life?

Physical

Spiritual

Eternal

How are the three types of life related
to each other?

Physical

Spiritual

Eternal

How might you use what you've learned in this chapter to help others in the years to come?

Quality Parents

You have been chosen as the guest speaker for a national parenting conference. The assigned title for your speech is: "Qualities of a Good Parent." Your speech must include five main points. The group knows you are a committed Christian, and everyone expects that you will use Scripture as the foundation of your message.

Outline your speech below. Include your main points and a brief example illustrating how parents can put each principle into practice. See **Deuteronomy 6:4-9, Ephesians 6:4, and Colossians 3:21** for some ideas to get you started.

When you're done, **circle the one trait you want to practice** as a future parent and then make sure you take time to affirm your own parent(s) (or those serving as your parents) for any areas of strength that they have displayed.

cre·ate (e) Pronunciation (
tr.v. cre·at·ed, cre·at·ing, cre·
1. To cause to exis
bring into being. 2. T
give rise to; produce
To produce through

Qualities of a Good Parent

1.

2.

3.

4.

5.

A little extra
When you know your parents' phone won't be
answered and will go directly to voicemail, leave
them an encouraging message and list the good
qualities they possess.

Plan Ahead

Look back at the qualities for parenting you listed on the last page. Read those Scripture passages again and write out some specific things you can do now to prepare yourself to be a good parent.

Preparing for Parenting

1.

2.

3.

4.

5.

All parents, including yours, acquired many of their qualities from their parenting experiences. Your parents may not be perfect, but they do have some positive qualities. Write your parents a letter on a separate sheet of paper thanking them for their love and acknowledging some of their positive qualities.

A little extra

Start a great dinner conversation by asking your parents what their lives were like as kids. Ask them about their **favorite memories,** and see how long you can keep them answering your questions.

Freedom Behind Bars

Read the verses on the topic of forgiveness listed on the right side of this page. Then write a letter to a fictitious prisoner who is serving a life sentence on a murder charge. The prisoner doesn't believe that God will forgive him even though he has put his faith in Jesus as Lord and Savior. **The purpose of your letter is to convince him of God's forgiveness.** Support your position with Scripture.

1 John 1:9; Ephesians 4:32; Mark 3:28-30; Romans 4:7-8

Consider this:

- 140,610 individuals serving life sentences right now
- 6,807 of them were juveniles at the time of the crime
- 41,095 serving have no possibility of parole
- 1,755 of those were juveniles at the time of the crime

[source: Community.nicic.org/blogs/corrections_headlines]

Don't be afraid to share your letter with a real person or prisoner (maybe a friend who has had an abortion or a family member who served time for a crime).

Jesus forgives the repentant heart completely.

Your Serve

Jesus came to earth as a servant and desired to leave his mark of servanthood on this world. *For even the Son of Man came not to be served but to serve others and to give his life as a ransom for many (Mark 10:45).*

Read John 13:1-20. Jesus chose this form of service to communicate servanthood to his disciples. What are some creative ways you can serve the significant people in your life today (such as washing the dishes without being told, conserving hot water for a sibling's shower, or getting up to refill drinks at a fast food restaurant)? **List your decisions for service below.**

How are you going to serve these people today?

Parents -

Brothers/sisters -

Friends -

Neighbors -

Teachers -

Employer -

49

assimore difficult, but it's information and appl

Heavy Weight

In **Psalm 38**, David pleads for God's mercy in his troubles and seeks God's deliverance from all his wrongful acts. *My guilt overwhelms me—it is a burden too* **HEAVY** *to bear (Psalm 38:4).*

To get a deeper understanding of what David meant, try this. Take a large pillowcase and fill it with books (such as textbooks, dictionaries, and cookbooks). Once filled, carry the pillowcase around during your daily chores or activities. It will be difficult and frustrating, but what you may learn could make the struggle worthwhile.

After completing the exercise, answer the following questions:

How might your sins be weighing you down like the pillowcase experience?

What three sins do you consistently struggle with?

cre·ate ( ) Pronunciation (
tr.v. cre·at·ed, cre·at·ing, cre·
1. To cause to exist
bring into being. 2. T
give rise to; produce
To produce throug

What friend or leader could you ask to help you overcome these sins?

In the space below, write a prayer asking God to forgive your sins, help you in your pursuit of him, and teach you a lasting lesson through your exercise.

If you really want to make this memorable, try sleeping with the burden pillow. Our sins don't go away just by sleeping them off.

Brand Name

Look through a magazine to find an advertisement that is selling a product that doesn't seem to relate to the photo. For example, you might find an ad selling deodorant that has a photo of a confident businessman sitting with a group of people. He's apparently confident because he uses this particular brand of deodorant.

Advertisers appeal to emotions with the hope to provoke a favorable response and loyalty for their product. Often the emotional (and/or visual) appeal has little or nothing to do with the product that is being sold. This subtle form of manipulation is a strategy companies use, hoping consumers like you and me will be drawn to the image and associate it with their brand.

It's Marketing 101.

Read Romans 12:3. Read it several times and consider what it might mean to you. Then, in the space below, create a brand name and a label design that accurately describes you. (An example of a made-up brand name might be "Uniquecre"—a composite of unique and creative—representing a desire to be different from the norm and creative in living.) Then explain why you chose your brand name and design.

A little habit-forming tip: Every time you read God's Word, consider making a news headline for the verse or verses you read. When you read the Bible, take mental notes of the voices in the story, the smells, sounds, and environment.

Pray Your Cards Right

Jesus said, *"But when you pray, go away by yourself, shut the door behind you, and pray to your Father in private. Then your Father, who sees everything, will reward you" (Matthew 6:6).*

Take a deck of playing cards into your prayer time today. Shuffle the deck and begin to lay the cards face up one-by-one until you have turned over four from the same suite (all spades, hearts, diamonds, or clubs). With each card you turn, offer a sentence prayer following this pattern:

When you turn over a heart say a prayer of thankfulness.

When you turn over a spade ask for forgiveness in an area of your life.

When you turn over a diamond pray for your dreams, goals, and future.

When you turn over a club pray for your family, your youth group, or another organization you belong to.

Grand Entrance

Sin separated humanity from God. In order to bridge the sin gap, God chose to send his only Son, Jesus Christ, to the earth so that we might be reunited with God.

If you were the God of the universe, how would you have chosen for your Son Jesus to make his entrance into the world? (For example, I might have had Jesus come out of the sky during the middle of the Super Bowl when much of the world was watching.)

Read Matthew 1:18-25 and Luke 2:1-20 to discover how Jesus did enter our world. How would you summarize Jesus' entrance?

Why do you think God chose for Jesus to come into the world the way he did?

Habit-forming tip:
When you read the Bible, ask yourself—if you were that character in the Bible, how would you have responded or acted in that situation?

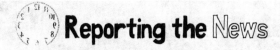

Reporting the News

Imagine that you are a news journalist covering the event of Jesus' triumphal entry into Jerusalem. Your story may be broadcast on the 6 o'clock news or hit the front page of the Jerusalem Daily Pilot.

Read the facts in **Matthew 21:1-22** and pretend that you are on the scene. As you write your story be sure to include Jesus' activities at the Temple, the significance of the fig tree, and the reaction of the crowd. Hope to see you on the news!

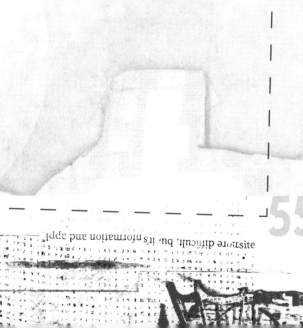

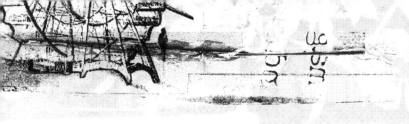

Thanks for Me

Psalm 139 explains that God sees all and knows everything about us. Verses 13-16 reveal that God even knew us before we were born.

Read the entire psalm, paying special attention to verses 13-16. Then write a letter thanking God for his greatness. Include your gratitude for **God's creative design in making you.** Ask God to forgive you for the times you've complained about how you were created.

Dear God,

cre·ate (g) Pronunciation
tr.v. cre·at·ed, cre·at·ing, cre
1. To cause to exist
bring into being. 2. T
give rise to; produce
To produce throu

A Word From the Sponsor

Below on the left is a list of five "channels" representing different elements of the Christian faith. On the right are five different "commercials" (verses) that belong to the five channels. Read the commercial references and match them with the correct channels.

Channels	Commercials
Forgiveness	1 Corinthians 12:4-6
Salvation	1 John 1:9
Eternal Life	John 3:3-8
Spiritual Gifts	Acts 1:8
Witnessing	John 3:36

Which commercial captures your attention at this time of your life? Why?

A little extra:

Spend **10 fewer minutes** in front of the TV or online today. Take this commercial challenge: An important part of *Creative Times With God* is the idea of "time." There is plenty of time to live God's way... God made all the time we need... It's up to us how we use and prioritize our time. Spend those 10 minutes completely alone with God.

Very Tempting

Read **Luke 4:1-13,** which describes the `temptations` Jesus faced in the desert. Then complete the following exercises.

Look up the word **"temptation"** in the dictionary or online at dictionary.com and write a definition in your own words here:

List `three temptations` that currently give you the greatest difficulty (for example: money, seeking popularity by conforming to the crowd, sex, cheating, and so on). Write them out as large as you can on this page. No matter how **BIG** the `temptation`, **God can free you from what enslaves you.**

1.

2.

3.

Write out 1 Corinthians 10:13. How does this verse **give you hope** for the temptations you face?

Express thanks that **God knows all** the temptations and feelings you experience.

Money Matters

Jesus talked a lot about money and wealth, and some of what he taught is very difficult to hear—in fact, many Christ-followers pretend not to hear and/or understand it. Read Jesus' words on wealth in **Luke 12:13-21.**

```
List five things you own that give you the
greatest satisfaction.


   1.

   2.

   3.

   4.

   5.


   Now, next to each item write what you
   think this thing will mean to you 10
   years from now.
```

Ask God to help you make the right decisions with your money and possessions because "a person is a fool to store up earthly wealth but not have a rich relationship with God" (Luke 12:21).

No Worries

On the previous page you read about riches in **Luke 12:13-21.** Following that section of Scripture, Jesus talked to his disciples about worrying—an issue many people still struggle with today.

Read what Jesus said about worrying in Luke 12:22-31.

o outside and find a flower, a leaf, or a blade of grass and
eep it with you until tomorrow. Every time you look at it or
eel it in your pocket, say a quick prayer of thanksgiving
or God's provision for you.

If you need to be more thankful

during your week, remember the

lilies and rejoice that "your Father

already knows your needs"

(Luke 12:30)

s more difficult, bu. it's nformation and appl

Table Talk

Move to the kitchen or dining room table to complete this exercise. Think of **five items** that are often on the table you're sitting at, such as a knife, a napkin, or a saltshaker. List them in the column on the left.

Then think of a verse or spiritual truth that each object suggests to you. For example, a knife may suggest Hebrews 4:12: *For the word of God is alive and powerful. It is sharper than the sharpest two-edged sword…* Or a napkin may remind you that God wipes away your sin when you seek forgiveness. Jot your ideas in the column on the right. Do your best to find a verse for each, but if you can't, don't worry about it.

Each time you use these items at the table this week, thank God for the truth they represent.

Table Object

1.

2.

3.

4.

5.

Truth It Represents

1.

2.

3.

4.

5.

cre·ate ( ) Pronunciation (k)
tr.v. cre·at·ed, cre·at·ing, cre·ates
1. To cause to exist;
bring into being. 2. T
give rise to; produce
To produce through

Lame Excuses

Read John 5:1-13. Notice the excuse the sick man used in verse 7 to defend his condition. If this story happened today, what kinds of excuses might the man use to explain why he hadn't taken advantage of God's provisions? **List five possible excuses below (be creative and humorous if you like).**

Excuses
1.

2.

3.

4.

5.

Now write down the names of three people you know who are making lame excuses for the condition of their relationships with God. Take time to pray for each of them, asking God to heal them like Jesus healed the sick man at the pool.

People
1.

2.

3.

Now that you have thought about others, think about yourself—are you offering any lame excuses that you need to confess to God?

How are you going to deal with excuses?

What is your next step? Do it. No more excuses.

 **Prayer Pattern**

In Matthew 6:9-13 Jesus gave his disciples an example of prayer that we call "the Lord's Prayer." He didn't say, "Always pray these words," but rather he instructed them to "Pray like this" (Matthew 6:9). Look at the Lord's Prayer as a style of praying instead of a required prayer that must be recited the same way each time.

Below are the phrases of the Lord's Prayer from the very famous and familiar King James Version. Pray through each phrase and make it personal to you.

"Our Father which art in heaven, Hallowed be thy name."

Spend some time praising and thanking God for his fatherly characteristics and holy name.

"Thy kingdom come, Thy will be done in earth, as it is in heaven."

Now is a good time to pray for God's will to be done in your life and in the lives of your family and friends.

"Give us this day our daily bread."

Pray now that God would feed you spiritually as you read the Bible.

"And forgive us our debts, as we forgive our debtors."

Ask God for personal forgiveness. Then ask God to remind you of people you need to forgive.

"And lead us not into temptation, but deliver us from evil."

Pray now for God to protect you from things that tempt you.

"For thine is the kingdom, and the power, and the glory, forever. Amen."

Conclude your prayer as you began it with praise to God for his greatness.

Holy Moses

Moses was a man God used in mighty ways to lead the Israelites out of Egyptian captivity and torture and guide them into the Promised Land. Read Exodus 3:1–4:17 to discover how God called Moses to this adventuresome task. **Then answer the questions below.**

How do you think God would most want to use you?

What great mission could you see yourself taking on for God?

Describe in detail below what you would like to do for God. Then write a prayer asking God to start preparing you to do his work in his time. But instead of writing a prayer where you are, go to your kitchen or bathroom sink and turn on the water as you write the prayer. Think about how a waterfall starts from a single drop of rain.

How might you be a drop in what God is doing?

cre·ate (e) Pronunciation (k...)
tr.v. cre·at·ed, cre·at·ing, cre...
1. To cause to exist; bring into being. *2.* To give rise to; produce. To produce through...

Missionary Journey

The Book of Acts reveals in splendid detail how the early church was birthed and quickly grew to reach thousands of people. The Apostle Paul and his friends traveled to different cities to preach the good news about Jesus, help new Christians, and plant churches. We refer to Paul's travels as missionary journeys. Read Acts 13:2-3 to see how these journeys began.

Get a map of your community and highlight key areas that need to be reached for Jesus (schools, government offices, housing complexes, and so on). Spend some time in prayer for each area you highlighted. Then answer the following questions:

What would be your strategy to reach each of these areas?

What is the possibility that you could actually do something like this in your community?

Who would you want to take with you? Why?

What kind of person do you think God would call to do something like this? What needs to happen to make you this kind of person?

What three words best represent reaching others for Christ? With a black marker write these words on the bottom of your shoes and pray as you do that. Ask God to lead you and give you exactly what you need to share his love with others.

Straight and Narrow

Your youth group wants to start a Bible club on campus next semester, and you've been asked to help provide leadership. But during final exams, a week before the new semester begins, you discover that your grades may not be good enough for you to serve as the school representative for a campus club. After figuring your GPA, you discover that you need A's on your last two finals. Your best grades so far have been B's.

You don't want to disappoint your youth group, but you know you'll never be a club rep next semester—unless you cheat on those last two exams. You sit next to straight-A students in both classes, and you know you could pull it off without getting caught.

What will you do?

Read the following verses to see how they might help you in this challenging situation: **Exodus 20:15; Proverbs 10:2; 12:5; 14:2; 15:16; Romans 7:18-25; Galatians 6:7; 1 Thessalonians 4:6; and 1 John 2:6.**

Write an honest letter to your youth group explaining your situation and describing what you will do. Be honest. Maybe you would choose to cheat… write that out. Then, regardless of what you write, take time to reflect on those Scriptures, your thoughts, and your future.

Dear friends,

 **Train Stop**

Read Galatians 6:10. Then imagine that you have access to four trains. Each train is loaded with one of the following qualities, and the trains are ready to distribute them at your direction:

Godliness

Honesty

Security

Laughter

You happen to know about four cities that are having problems. Each city needs one of the above trains to remedy its situation. Read each description below and decide which of the four trains should be sent there. **Write your decision beneath each description and explain the reason for your selection.**

City #1
This city has gone downhill ever since the new mayor was elected. He is trying to pass laws that will make his office and staff look good. But his laws are doing nothing for the good of the city. People are angry, but they lack the power to pressure the mayor to change.

Decision:
Reason:

City #2

The people in City #2 don't know what to do about all the crime that is going on in their community. Homes are being burglarized, schools are being vandalized, and stores are going out of business because of robbery and theft. The police department is too small to stop all the wrongdoing.

Decision:
Reason:

City #3

No one seems to care in this city. There is no public participation in any activities. The churches are empty, the parks are deserted, and no one attends civic planning meetings. Kids don't play outside after school, neighbors don't talk to each other, and people are chained to their jobs.

Decision:
Reason:

cre·ate (e) Pronunciation (k)
tr.v. *cre·at·ed, cre·at·ing, cre*
1. To cause to exist
bring into being. 2. T
give rise to; produce
To produce through

City #4

People have been living in this city for many years. Families are strong and community relationships are good. But unemployment is a serious problem. Some people must travel over 100 miles each way to work. And those who do work in the city earn very little because of the depressed economy.

Decision:
Reason:

This was a fairly easy task, but it's not so easy when it's about your life. **Take some time to reflect on your own life and make this question personal to you.**

Which of these four trains would you need most at your house? Why?

To Sum Up...

Summarize each of the verses below in five words or less, and then complete the activity at the end.

Verse 1: "You were dead because of your sins and because your sinful nature was not yet cut away. Then God made you alive with Christ, for he forgave all our sins" (Colossians 2:13).
Verse 1 Summary:

Verse 2: "But if we confess our sins to him, he is faithful and just to forgive us our sins and to cleanse us from all wickedness " (1 John 1:9).
Verse 2 Summary:

Verse 3: "If you forgive those who sin against you, your heavenly Father will forgive you. But if you refuse to forgive others, your Father will not forgive your sins" (Matthew 6:14-15).
Verse 3 Summary:

The main point of these verses is...

On a separate sheet of paper write a list of sins in your life that you know need to be forgiven. Ask God to cleanse you from these sins. After praying, tear up the sheet of paper and throw it away, symbolizing how God forgives your sins. Then reread Matthew 6:14-15 and consider the warning from this passage.

Reaching In

In **1 Corinthians 9:19-23** Paul explains and illustrates how he was willing to do anything in order to share the good news about Jesus. Read these verses to appreciate Paul's commitment to extend himself to the various people-groups in his world.

In the column on the left list two groups at your school that you are currently not connected to (for example: a drama group, sports team, party crowd). Then, consider a strategy for how you might reach out to people in those two groups and involve them in your church or youth group. Write your creative strategies on the right. If the task seems difficult to you, remember Paul's words: **For I can do everything through Christ, wh gives me strength (Philippians 4:13).**

Groups to Reach	Strategies for Reaching
1.	A. B. C.
2.	A. B. C.

A little extra:

Paul learned other people's "language" by studying their culture and then spoke to them from their perspective. What is a group that you currently don't understand? (Examples: People who love country music, gamers, jocks, and so on.) How might you learn to speak their language? And why might that be important?

International Intercession

Find a map of the world on the Internet and select a country you don't know much about. Gather some information about this country—per capita income, infant mortality rate, life expectancy, economic structure, and so on.

Then search out information in the same categories for the United States. How do the two countries compare? What are some of the needs you see in the foreign country you studied?

Read 1 Timothy 2:1-4 and pray for this country. Pray for its government, economy, Christians and churches, health needs, and family structures. Complete the following statements to help direct your prayers:

My country is...

I will remember to pray for this
country when I see...

I will pray for...

Wise Guys

Read Proverbs 2:1-22. List the key words that are used most often in this chapter here:

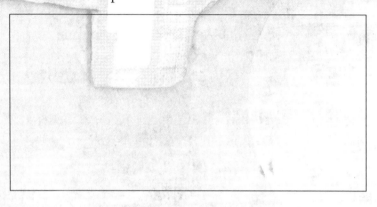

1 What do you find special or interesting about these words?

2 How can these words help bring wisdom into your life?

cre·ate (e) Pronunciation (
tr.v. cre·at·ed, cre·at·ing, cre
1. To cause to exist
bring into being. 2.
give rise to; produce
To produce throu

3 Describe one situation where you need God's wisdom today. How does Proverbs 2:6 help you face that situation?

4 According to this chapter, how does a person receive wisdom?

5 Among your friends and family members, who especially needs to hear these ideas on wisdom? When will you share these thoughts with this person?

Personal Policy

Ask a parent to show you a copy of an insurance policy. Look through it and notice that the policy protects certain possessions. Each policy insures the specific possessions the policyholder wants to protect (such as a home, a car, a boat, or a wedding ring).

Today you are the policyholder and you get to write a policy that protects four people and/or possessions that are of great value to you. Follow the example to describe the items or people you want protected, why each is special to you, and what each one's value is to you.

Personal Insurance Policy

What I Want Protected	Why it is Special	Its Value
1. Cathy	She is my wife. I value our friendship, her love, and the way she makes me feel. She is the joy of my life!	Irreplaceable
2.		
3.		

Personal Insurance Policy

What I Want Protected	Why it is Special	Its Value
4.		
5.		

Read Deuteronomy 4:31. How well-protected do you feel as God's possession?

Digging Deeper

Read 1 Peter 3:15. If people at school asked you why you're a follower of Jesus, could you provide a good answer? What if they started asking questions that needed answers beyond simply saying,

"I just take it by faith"

List on the next page some questions about God and/or faith for which you don't have answers. Spend some time in the next few weeks trying to find answers to these questions. Ask a pastor, research online, or consult a friend who knows more about the Christian faith than you do.

As you research these questions, ask God to lead you to helpful resources. Be sure to share the results of your search with a friend or family member.

Some examples might be: **Why do bad things happen to good people? Why isn't everything black/white in the Bible? Why is there evil if God is a good God?**

Question 1:

Answers:

Question 2:

Answers:

Question 3:

Answers:

Question 4:

Answers:

Kid Power

In Luke 9:46-48 Jesus settled a squabble about who was the greatest—and his closest followers were arguing this question. Jesus illustrated his answer by using a child, and in doing so, he taught some important truths about power.

Look through a magazine and clip a few photos of some powerful people in our world. Tape these pictures on the left side of the space below.

Also clip some photos of babies or young children and tape them on the right side of the space.

Then answer the questions on the next page.

cre·ate (ɛ) Pronunciation (kr
tr.v. cre·at·ed, cre·at·ing, cre·a
1. To cause to exist
bring into being. 2. T
give rise to; produce
To produce throu

What are the differences between the two groups of people pictured?

What main points was Jesus illustrating when he used a little child as an example?

How would your life be different if you had more power?

Find a diaper, baby bottle, or child's toy and place it where you will regularly see it over the next few days. Let it remind you of Jesus' perspective on power and the importance of childlikeness in God's kingdom.

Habit-forming tip:

When you read your Bible, consider finding images from a magazine that might illustrate the verses you've been reading. Put them in your Bible, and soon your Bible will become a visual reference and memory tool.

Marked Events

Many of Jesus' significant miracles and teachings are recorded in the Gospel of Mark. Below is a list of 16 events—one from each chapter. Search through the Gospel of Mark to discover the chapter where each is found. (It's easier than you might think!)

Circle the event that is most meaningful to you at this point in your life and write a brief summary explaining its significance. Try to memorize these locations for future reference.

Chapter	Event
☐	Jesus feeds the 5,000
☐	Jesus is asked, "What is the greatest commandment?"
☐	Temptation of Jesus
☐	Jesus casts demons out of a man and into swine
☐	Jesus meets the rich young man
☐	The paralytic is lowered through the roof and healed
☐	The transfiguration
☐	The resurrection of Jesus
☐	The Last Supper
☐	Jesus talks about the end times
☐	Jesus appoints the 12 disciples
☐	Peter's confession of Christ
☐	The crucifixion of Jesus
☐	Jesus heals a girl possessed by a demon
☐	The triumphal entry
☐	Jesus calms the storm

Jesus feeds the 5,000
Jesus is asked, "What is the greatest commandment?"
Temptation of Jesus
Jesus casts demons out of a man and into swine
Jesus meets the rich young man
The paralytic lowered through the roof and healed
The transfiguration
The resurrection of Jesus
The Last Supper
Jesus talks about the end times
Jesus appoints the 12 disciples
Peter's confession of Christ
The crucifixion of Jesus
Jesus heals a girl possessed by a demon
The triumphal entry
Jesus calms the storm

A little extra:

Create your own stick figure theater. It's really easy. Pick one event from the previous page. Now, draw three boxes. Draw a stick figure in each box. Draw a talking bubble by each figure. Fill the first bubble with an event that is meaningful to you. Fill in the next bubble with why it's meaningful to you. Fill in the last bubble with the reference in Mark.

Wonder Woman

Read Proverbs 31:10-31, a thorough description of a woman who possesses godly qualities that make her shine with inner beauty.

If you're a girl, write down five qualities from this passage that inspire you. Next to each quality write a goal that will help you continue to develop that quality or an idea of how you might grow in that particular area.

-FEMALE-

Qualities	Goals
1.	1.
2.	2.
3.	3.
4.	4.
5.	5.

cre·ate (e) Pronunciation ( )
tr.v. cre·at·ed, cre·at·ing, cre
1. To cause to exist
bring into being. 2. T
give rise to; produce
To produce throu

If you're a guy, write down five qualities that you would most like to see in the woman you marry. Then rank those qualities from one to five in order of their importance, with number one being the most important. Ask God to prepare you to be the kind of man who will bring out the inner beauty in your future wife.

-MALE-

Qualities	Order of Importance
1.	1.
2.	2.
3.	3.
4.	4.
5.	5.

Guys: Write down ways you can bring out these qualities in a future wife or even the girls you hang around.

Ladies: Write down ways you can bring out these qualities in a future husband or even the guys you hang around.

Radio Waves

Listen to your favorite radio station for 10 minutes. As you listen, write or type the themes, words, and messages you hear—both positive and negative.

Positive : Negative

What do you feel is positive about the music you listen to?

What do you feel is negative about your music or your favorite station? What do others suggest is negative about it?

Are you aware of any controversies over Christian and/or non-Christian music in your church or community? If so, what are the issues surrounding the controversy?

What is your opinion on those issues?

Read Ephesians 5:19-20. What kind of music do you think should be included in a Christian's music diet? Why?

A little extra:
Search for your favorite song or group on iTunes. Click on the album and then look on the right-hand side to see what albums were also purchased by people who bought this particular album. Is there a trend showing up in similar music or artists? Are you surprised by the other albums purchased based on your favorite music?

Giving a Compass

Dear brothers and sisters, if another believer is overcome by some sin, you who are godly should gently and humbly help that person back onto the right path. And be careful not to fall into the same temptation yourself (Galatians 6:1).

Why do you think the Apostle Paul stresses **"gently and humbly"** in this verse?

What should you do if a follower of Jesus continues in the same sin and refuses your efforts to be restored? (Read Matthew 18:15-17.)

Do you know a struggling Christian who **needs to be encouraged** in his/her faith? Take some time to pray for that person. Also pray that God will help you stay on the right path.

- -

What specific things can you do to help your friend get back on the right path? List a few ideas below.

1.

- -

2.

- -

3.

When can you try some of these things? Come back to this verse later and report back what happened.

# We've Got Spirit

Write a brief paragraph explaining your current understanding of the Holy Spirit.

Often the role of the Holy Spirit is misunderstood and he is viewed as some type of mystical ghost or wizard who acts on behalf of God. **Look up the following verses and make notes on what the Bible teaches about the Holy Spirit.**

What are the Holy Spirit's feelings?

Romans 15:30

Ephesians 4:30

Hebrews 10:29

What are the Holy Spirit's thoughts?
John 14:26

Romans 8:26-27

1 Corinthians 2:10-11

What are the Holy Spirit's desires?
Acts 13:2

John 16:8-11

Write a new paragraph summarizing what you have learned from reading about the Holy Spirit.

cre·ate (ɛ) Pronunciation (k
tr.v. cre·at·ed, cre·at·ing, cre
1. To cause to exis
bring into being. 2. T
give rise to; produce
To produce throu

 **Comic Relief**

Grab your Bible and some comic books or cartoons
from a newspaper.

1. Look for a comic that illustrates a Bible verse or Bible
story. Cut it out, write the verse reference on it, and tape it
someplace where you will regularly see it.

2. Look for a comic that represents something going on in your
life or a friend's life. Cut it out and give to your friend with an
encouraging note—or place it where you'll see it and write out
what it inspires you to do (or stop doing).

3. Cut out a cartoon that reminds you of a friend or family
member. Send it to him or her with an encouraging note or Bible
verse.

4. Draw your own cartoon on a separate sheet of paper for your
youth pastor. Make sure it's encouraging!

5. Illustrate a favorite Bible verse in cartoon form. Then share it
with a family member.

6. Find a humorous YouTube video and send the link to a friend,
along with a Bible verse that might fit with the message of the
video—keep it encouraging.

Dear Me

In Revelation 2 and 3, Jesus Christ dictated seven `letters` to the Apostle John to be delivered to the churches in Ephesus, Smyrna, Pergamum, Thyatira, Sardis, Philadelphia, and Laodicea. (Say that three times fast!) These `letters` contained both encouragement and challenges to the Christians in these cities. Read at least two of these `letters` before continuing this exercise.

If God decided to write you today, what would the `letter` say?

Go ahead and write this letter as you think it might appear. Be sure to include both encouragement and challenge.

Dear (*your name*),

`A little extra:`
E-mail the letter to your parents and ask them if they agree with the letter. Why do they agree, or why don't they agree?

I'm Thankful!

Be thankful today! You have many reasons to be thankful, no matter what situation you may be facing. Try to think of 26 specific reasons to be thankful, using each letter of the alphabet. It will be a challenge, but with a little thought you will be able to do it. **Before you start, read 1 Thessalonians 5:18 and Ephesians 5:20.**

A-

B-

C-

D-

E-

F-

G-

H-

I-

J-

K-

L-

M-

N-

O-

P-

Q-

R-

S-

T-

U-

V-

W-

X-

Y-

Z-

Making Money Count

1 Timothy 6:6-10 contains wise words of warning concerning the love of money. Read these verses slowly and carefully. Evaluate where you stand in relation to the warnings presented. Could these words be speaking directly to you about your current view of money—or possibly a warning for the future? **Ask God to teach you something this week about money.**

Take out a dollar bill, lay it out on the next page, and trace around it. Then divide the dollar-sized rectangle into three sections. Give each section one of the following headings:

```
(1) Why I like money
(2) How money affects me
(3) How God views money
```

Fill each section with your written response to the heading. Then pray that God will give you a proper perspective on money.

Chaos & Conflict

Read about the conflict between Paul and Barnabas in Acts 15:36-41. These servants of God were on a missionary journey planting churches and encouraging followers of Jesus. It was a great mission, yet they had a major conflict. But they resolved the conflict and continued their individual ministries with new partners.

Answer the following questions about conflicts in your life:

Do you have a conflict with someone in your life? If so, describe the nature of the conflict.

Have you completely resolved this conflict? If so, how did you do it? If not, what can you do today to help solve the problem?

Read Matthew 5:21-26 and Ephesians 4:26-27.
What do these verses teach you about handling conflicts with people in your life?

Run Feet Run!

In his letters to Timothy, the Apostle Paul instructs his young friend Timothy to run away from evil practices. Read Paul's words in **1 Timothy 6:6-11 and 2 Timothy 2:22.** Then answer the following:

Why do you think Paul warns Timothy to stay away from evil practices?

What are some temptations that Paul might warn you to run from? List them here.

How might these evil practices affect you in the future if you don't follow Paul's advice?

What are some specific ways you can run from each of the evils you listed above?

What's Your Isaac?

God tested Abraham's faith by instructing him to present his son Isaac, whom he loved more than anything, as a human sacrifice. **Read the story in Genesis 22:1-18.**

God wanted to see which was more important in Abraham's life—his son Isaac or his obedience to God. After Abraham proved himself, God told him, "I will certainly bless you … all because you have obeyed me" (Genesis 22:17a, 18b).

Let's say that the "Isaacs" in our lives are those people and things that rival God for our attention. List the "Isaacs" that can tempt you to be considered more important than God. On the right side, write out why each "Isaac" is or is not more important to you than God at this time.

My Isaacs are...	More important than God? Why or why not?
1.	
2.	
3.	
4.	
5.	

bring into being. 2. give rise to; produce To produce

 **Has Jesus Gone Mad?**

Read Mark 11:15-26. Then answer the following questions:

Is it difficult for you to imagine Jesus angry? Why or why not?

What kinds of situations would make Jesus angry today?

What makes you angry?

How do you express your anger? Do you consider your expression of anger a healthy expression? Why or why not?

What can you do this week to improve the way you deal with anger?

Write some ways you can apply this verse to your life: *And "don't sin by letting* anger *control you." Don't let the sun go down while you are still* angry *(Ephesians 4:26).*

Read this verse again later in the week. It's one thing to say "Don't sin," and it's another to actually not sin. Did you get angry this week? What happened? Did the verse come to mind when you got angry? What did you do: obey or ignore?

Hope for a Rainbow

The biblical account of the great flood ends with God's promise confirmed by the sign of a rainbow. Ever since, the rainbow has been a beautiful symbol of hope. Read God's hope-filled promise in Genesis 9:8-17.

Imagine that one end of a colorful rainbow rests on your church. You have the opportunity to place the other end of the rainbow **anywhere in your community that needs a ray of hope**—your school, the local hangout, a rough part of town, or some other place. Where would you like to see the rainbow settle? Write your answer in the space below. Then make a list of creative ways you and your youth group can bring hope to that section of your community.

A rainbow of hope is needed at:

Some ideas for bringing hope to this area are...

1.

2.

3.

4.

5.

Stranded on a Deserted Island

Imagine that you are

stranded

on a deserted island with four other people. Your basic needs for food and shelter are supplied, but you have no hope of ever leaving the island.

The others look to you as the spiritual leader, but you don't even have a Bible on the island. You decide to write a simple constitution to govern how you will live on the island based on principles you remember from the Bible.

Use Romans 12:18 as the goal for writing your version of a constitution below.

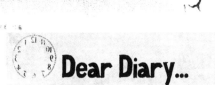 **Dear Diary...**

Take a moment to think through your past year or two. Regardless of your age, this is an exercise that can be practiced annually. Write out your answers to the following questions:

What's the funniest thing that happened to you during the last year?

List the top three memories of the year and the three memories you wish you could forget.

Take a moment to thank God for the positive memories, and write out some lessons learned from the not-so-hot memories.

List two or three things that currently worry or concern you.

Read Matthew 6:25-34 and complete this sentence: I know I don't need to worry about life because...

Try writing your answers as well as some of your prayers. **Then try something a little different**—or attach your written prayers to something around the house that you don't see all the time— like a box of new light bulbs or tools in the garage. When it comes time to replace a bulb or use the tools, revisit the list. **Are your prayers being answered?**

cre·ate (e) Pronunciation (
tr.v. cre·at·ed, cre·at·ing, cre·
1. To cause to exist
bring into being. 2. T
give rise to; produce
To produce through

 # My Version

Select a short psalm or a collection of proverbs from the Old

Testament. Write the psalm or the proverbs in your own words,

being sure to make it your own unique (and creative) version

of what you read. Use names of people you know, locations in

your community, and situations that are common to you. After

doing this, you may find yourself remembering this passage of

Scripture much longer because of the time you invest in trying

to understand it.

Distinguished Speaker

Imagine that you are the master of ceremonies at a banquet and Jesus is the scheduled speaker. Your job is to introduce Jesus to the audience by telling them who he is, what he has done, and why they should listen to him.

Write your introductory speech below. You may want to read some of the following verses to help you prepare your introduction: Matthew 1:23; John 6:51; Acts 3:15; 5:31; and Galatians 3:13.

Ladies and gentlemen, I would like to introduce Jesus, who...

The Master's Mail

Read 2 Corinthians 3:1-3, which describes followers of Jesus as living letters. These personal letters can be read by those watching their lives. Today, as a follower of Jesus, you are also a living letter of Christ. Write a letter to Jesus and explain in your letter how you are doing as a follower and why you are thankful for what he has done for you. Then tell Jesus what you are (or are not) doing now to display to others your love for him.

After completing your letter, seal it in an envelope, address it to yourself, and stamp it. Give the sealed envelope to a friend and ask him/her to hold it for several weeks before mailing it back to you. When the letter arrives, reread it and see how things may or may not have **changed in your life.**

 Flip for Prayer

Read Colossians 1:9-12 and notice Paul's commitment to pray for others. Then grab a coin and your family address book, school directory, or the contacts on your phone. Flip the coin to decide whom you will pray for today. If you flip "heads," turn to names beginning with A-L. For "tails," turn to names beginning with M-Z. Continue to flip the coin to narrow your choice to one name. Heads always designates the first half of the alphabet section you're working with, and tails always designates the second half.

When you have selected a name, **pray** for that person. After praying, you may want to write a short, encouraging **note** saying that you have prayed for him/her. Then send them a **text message** and let them know that you've been praying for them.

Person:_____
- [ ] Prayer
- [ ] Note
- [ ] Text

Person:_____
- [ ] Prayer
- [ ] Note
- [ ] Text

Person:_____
- [ ] Prayer
- [ ] Note
- [ ] Text

Person:_____
- [ ] Prayer
- [ ] Note
- [ ] Text

 **All-Stars**

Read Galatians 5:22-23 and think of the nine fruit of the Spirit as players on a team. From these nine select the three top all-stars you would like on your team. Write them in the appropriate spaces below.

Then write a brief, descriptive introduction of each all-star explaining why that quality is important to your team.

All-Star Number One:

All-Star Number Two:

All-Star Number Three:

Family Feuds

You'll find problems in homes all over the world—problems and conflicts are part of life. Conflicts occur between husbands and wives, parents and children, and brothers and sisters. Harmony in the home is almost impossible to achieve.

List up to five common problems that occur among family members today. Next to each problem describe how you think Jesus would respond to each one. Use Scripture references to support your comments wherever possible.

Family Problems	How Jesus Might Respond
1.	1.
2.	2.
3.	3.
4.	4.
5.	5.

cre·ate ( ) Pronunciation (
tr.v. cre·at·ed, cre·at·ing, cre
1. To cause to exist
bring into being. 2. T
give rise to; produce
To produce throug

Imagine that you have been invited to write a policy for peace for families and homes of the world. Write your peace policy below based on what you think Jesus might write.

Poor Me

Pretend that you are a high school student in Ecuador. Your mother and father both work full-time jobs to put food on the table. As a teenager you work five hours every day after school and 12 hours on the weekend to help your family's financial situation. You wear the same clothes to school every day because of your family's poverty.

You recently won an academic award, and your government is sending you to the United States to spend a week with an American family. In this "pretend" situation, the family you will stay with is your actual family. You will need to adjust to the living standards and amenities that your real family enjoys. How do you think you would respond to your house, parents, friends, and lifestyle?

On the next page, write a letter to your parents in Ecuador describing what you like and don't like about American family life. Also explain what you are learning through the experience.

Dear Mom and Dad,

The United States is not like Ecuador because...

Read Philippians 4:11-13. Then write a note of thanks for what God has given you. Share your letter with your "real" parents and see what type of discussion follows.

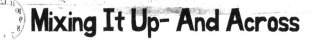

Mixing It Up- And Across

You won't find this crossword puzzle as difficult as the ones in the newspaper, but the answers will be more meaningful to you. **Give it a try.**

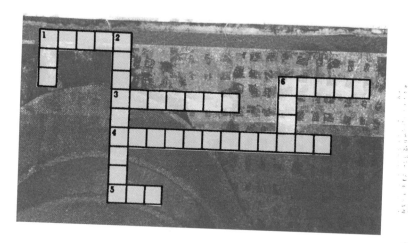

Across

1. This man is given many names and titles in the Bible.
3. This is the _____ that has overcome the world, even our faith (1 John 5:4 NIV).
4. According to 1 Thessalonians 5:18, we should have this in all circumstances.
5. Therefore, if anyone is in Christ, he is a new creation; the old has gone, the new has come! (2 Corinthians 5:17 NIV).
6. Jesus does this three times in Mark 5.

Down

1. The fruit of the Spirit is listed in Galatians 5:22-23. This is the only quality with three letters.
2. According to Ephesians 6:17 we are to take the helmet of _____.
6. What do we have as an anchor for the soul, according to Hebrews 6:19?

A little extra:

Redraw this crossword with sidewalk chalk in the church parking lot. Let others fill in the blanks so everyone can see it.

Handle with Care

Google the words "kitchen knives" and find a website where you can view different types of kitchen knives. List a few of them below, providing a brief explanation of each one's function.

Knife Function

1.

2.

3.

Read Hebrews 4:12 and list some ways God's Word can function like a sharp knife in your life.

1

2.

3.